MW00464955

Sammy Goes On Tour

Judy S. Walter

Layout and Design by
Penny Maxson

~ ~ ~ ~ ~

Printed in the USA

The journey begins as an idea in the mind. Then it is verbalized and discussed. From there a plan is developed. The date and itinerary are set. Finally, the day arrives and the journey begins.

This is a work of fiction.

Table of Contents

Chapter 1

Planning

SAMMY, THE TALKING CAT

Judy S. Walter

Over the past couple of years Sammy has become rather famous. Many people have come to know him through his book, <u>Sammy, The Talking Cat</u>. He has fans in many towns and states.

Because of this, the author and her sister Jenny have decided to take Sammy on tour. It's time for some of his fans to meet Mr. Personality.

Preparations for the tour got underway. First and foremost, a schedule had to be made, including book signings and hotel accommodations. Where to begin? A sit down meeting was arranged for Tuesday at Jenny's house.

"Where should we go?" asked Jenny.

"Somewhere with people and lots of food," Sammy replied. Everyone laughed at this.

"No doubt. And it must be places where I've sold books. Remember: this tour is for fans to meet Sammy," I said.

"Well, let's see. We need to make a list. Jenny, you write down the towns so we can look at the list and decide. We probably should start right here in Chambersburg."

Jenny and I collaborated and the final list was pretty extensive. We couldn't possibly visit all the places, but the list was something to look at and help us plan the trip. Here is the list.

Chambersburg, PA
Mercersburg, PA
McConnellsburg, PA
Waynesboro, PA
Gettysburg, PA
Walnut Bottom, PA
Carlisle, PA
Martinsburg, WV
Charleston, WV
Charlottesville, VA
Lumberton, NC
Dallas, TX

There were also some fans in California, Washington State, and Florida. We decided the West Coast was too far away, as was Florida. It was going to be a road trip, not a flight. Now, all we had to do was decide which towns to visit and start making the arrangements.

Sammy wanted to know if we could go all the way to Lumberton, North Carolina. Wow!

That would be a long time to keep a big boy in a carrier. And he would need potty breaks.

"What do you think, Jenny?"

"Well, we have to start in Chambersburg. He has so many local fans. Oh, wait. We forgot Scotland, PA. He has many fans there as well. And I think we need to visit Gettysburg. Now remember, you did sell a lot of books in Mercersburg also.

"Gettysburg and Mercersburg are in opposite directions," I said.

I could see this wasn't going to be easy. Maybe we should start at the farthest point – Lumberton - and work our way back home. Or maybe we should forget about Lumberton. Ohhh. Too many decisions. And what about Charleston, West Virginia? Sammy has a lot of fans there. One little girl even had her picture taken while holding Sammy's book.

Maybe we should get Jim's opinion. After all, he knew the roads.

"Why don't you start by eliminating places on the list? That way you'll have a shorter list to work with," Jim suggested.

At that point Sammy went running for his litter box. After he finished, Jenny had to scoop it so we could breathe comfortably.

"I'm sorry. It's just so nerve-wracking planning this tour and eliminating places." Poor Sammy.

OK. Time for a new list.

Chambersburg,PA
Scotland, PA
Walnut Bottom, PA
Carlisle, PA
Gettysburg, PA
Charleston, WV
Falling Waters, WV
Martinsburg, WV
Charlottesville, VA
Lumberton, NC

Now what? Who decides? Jenny will be driving; Sammy will be in his carrier. No one said anything. Finally, I made an executive decision. We would eliminate either Lumberton or Charleston.

"Ohhh." It was Sammy. "But I have fans in both places."

Jenny and I discussed the two towns and their relationship to other places on the tour. Eventually, we decided to eliminate Charleston, WV. Sammy had heard so much about Lumberton, NC, and he really wanted to go there. We could not disappoint him. After all, he was the celebrity.

Next, we decided to eliminate Carlisle and a couple of other towns too. Finally, the decision was made. Sammy's tour would include the following towns:

Chambersburg, PA
Gettysburg, PA
Lumberton, NC

The one issue with going to Gettysburg was that not all the fans who bought his book lived there. Gettysburg is a popular tourist town. Who knows where his fans may have been from?

Now that the towns were chosen, Sammy danced around like the proud celebrity he was. What a happy Boy!

Later that evening Jenny called me to say that Sammy had thought things over and was not happy. He felt that three towns were not enough for his tour. He wanted to visit more towns. Jenny and I decided to think about it for a few days.

Meanwhile, we would need to buy some things for Sammy's trip. He would need a harness and leash for sure. Of course, we would take his food and bottles of water along. Jenny said she would get a new litter pan to take into hotels.

I scheduled an appearance at the bookstore in Gettysburg for the following Saturday. The store manager said she would announce it on Facebook and issue a press release for the local newspaper. Sammy was excited. His Gettysburg fans would soon get to meet him.

The next morning Jenny called and told me that Sammy had whimpered half the night.

"What about?" I asked.

She said they went over the list again last night at his insistence. He wants to visit another one or two towns. She said he's really fretting over it.

"Well, we can't have the star of the tour fretting. Since they are on the way south, why don't we stop in Falling Waters, West Virginia and Martinsburg, West Virginia? Ask him if that will make him happy."

Later that evening Jenny called to say that Sammy finally approved of the tour. After all, five towns was a respectable number. She said that he even stopped pacing and took a nap. He was no longer stressed. Poor boy.

It's amazing how a little thing like the number of towns on a tour can affect a celebrity cat. I'll have to remember that for the next time. I guess five towns makes him feel more important than three.

Now back to the planning and scheduling of the actual trip. Appearances and hotels would have to be booked. I was still concerned about the long trip to Lumberton. We would just have to see how Sammy tolerated the trip.

Chapter 2

Gettysburg

Finally, the day came when Sammy was to meet his Gettysburg fans. The appearance was scheduled for 11 AM. We arrived fifteen minutes early, giving Sammy time for a potty break and time for Jenny to put his tie on him. She had bought him a red one because red is his favorite color and it looks good on him.

To our surprise, a news truck and photographer were waiting outside the store. Wow! How exciting for Sammy! He loved the attention. The photographer snapped several pictures of Sammy walking into the store on his leash. What a proud boy he was!

Susie, the store manager, was happy to finally meet him. After all, he had brought money into the store from the sales of his book. She gushed over him.

A table was set up for him near the front of the store along with several copies of his book, Sammy, The Talking Cat, for me to sign as they were purchased. Jenny held onto Sammy's leash to keep him safe. He was purring loudly and smiling.

"Look at that pretty cat," remarked a young woman who came through the door.

She couldn't believe his size. People continued to come in to meet the famous cat.

We were there for two hours, during which time I autographed about a dozen books. Everyone was happy. The photographer had long since vanished.

Sammy told his last visitor that he was glad to meet her, but he was tired. It was his nap time. Everyone laughed and Sammy yawned.

After we left the bookstore, Jenny and I decided to stop at our friend Alice's restaurant. She had good Chinese food. While Jenny was parking the car, I went in and asked if we could bring Sammy in.

"Sure. I've heard so much about him. Take the back booth so no one complains."

Sammy said he would take a nap while we ate. I ordered Chicken Chow Mein and egg drop soup. Jenny got Chicken and Vegetables and wonton soup. We shared a pot of tea. Lunch was delicious.

Sammy slept. In fact, he snored. He had had a big day. It was his first outing as a celebrity and he was no spring chicken. What a day it had been for him. His Gettysburg fans would not soon forget the big tiger cat who talked.

Jenny and I decided this would be a one day trip since it was Sammy's first appearance. He would have a couple of days to rest before we began our trip south for Sammy's celebrity tour. That would also give Jenny time to check supplies and make sure Sammy had enough food, water, and litter for the big trip.

Chapter 3

Falling Waters

Wednesday morning arrived – the day of our departure. Jenny and Sammy picked me up at my house. I said good-bye to Mitzi and loaded the trunk with Sammy's books and my suitcase. Sammy was in his carrier strapped in the back seat. Because it was a new car, Jenny had placed a blanket on the back seat under his carrier.

"Good morning, Aunt Judy."

"Are you ready for your big trip, Sammy?"

"You bet. I've been waiting for this trip for a long time."

"I'm so glad, Sammy. You deserve to meet your fans. It will be a great tour."

Our first planned stop was the rest area on I 81 South. We had decided to take Sammy out on the leash and save the litter box for the hotel. This proved to be a good plan, but we had to convince Sammy that it was OK to go potty outside.

Next, we headed to Falling Waters, WV, a small town not far off the interstate. We'd made arrangements with the Methodist Church for Sammy's appearance. I had sold a number of books there.

We were met by several of the church members. Sammy gave them a big smile as he walked into the social hall on his leash.

The show organizer (I sell books at their Christmas Show), some of the kitchen help as well as the pastor and his wife wanted their pictures taken with Sammy. They even had treats for him.

"Mom, may I eat a few treats?" he asked Jenny. "These people were nice enough to buy them for me."

"I guess a few won't hurt."

After the photos and treats, we took Sammy outside for a potty break before we said good-bye and got back into the car. It was time to continue on our journey.

Chapter 4

Martinsburg, WV

We continued on our way to Martinsburg to the VA Medical Center, where I had sold a lot of copies of Sammy's book. Jenny had called ahead and they were expecting us. We could not, however, go into the cafeteria area with Sammy. He was only allowed in the front lobby.

We pulled up at the entrance. I got out of the car and unfastened the door to Sammy's carrier. I hooked his leash to his collar. Then I put his red cape on him as well as his little tie.

Sammy jumped out of the car and started walking into the building. He was so regal looking. Jenny parked the car. We waited just inside the door for her to return.

When she arrived, I walked into the outer seating area for the cafeteria and announced that Sammy was here. Several people, including our friend Bill, said they wanted to meet him. They got up and followed me to the lobby.

Although he walked slowly, Bill was still the first person to greet Sammy. "Well, hello, young man," he said as he reached down to pet him.

Sammy winked at him. He could tell Bill liked him. He walked over to Bill and said, "You can hold me as long as you don't wrinkle my cape or tie." We all laughed, and Bill picked him up.

"You are one smart cat," Bill said. Sammy just smiled and purred.

Several other patients and hospital workers stopped to pet Sammy. Bill offered to get him a treat. We politely said no, that Sammy only ate his regular food – and plenty of that. We promised to give Sammy some when we got back to the car. We didn't tell Bill that Sammy got treats in Falling Waters earlier.

After about half an hour, Jenny said it was time to go. "We have a long drive ahead of us." Sammy said maybe he would take a nap after his snack.

Bill reluctantly handed him over to me after Jenny brought the car to the door. "Good-bye, Sammy. I'll never forget you. Have a nice trip." I could see that Bill needed a cat to keep him company.

We gave Sammy some snacks which were really his crunchy food. Then we hit the road.

Chapter 5

Continuing South

The trip south, although long, was uneventful. As was our custom, we stopped at ALL the rest areas. This gave Sammy plenty of opportunities for water and potty breaks. It also gave him a chance to stretch his legs so that he would not get stiff.

At one of the rest stops he asked if he could stay in the car and sleep. It was his nap time. So Jenny and I took turns using the restroom while the other one stayed in the car with Sammy. No way would we leave him alone. He's too important to be taken by a stranger. We both love him.

Since most of the restaurants do not allow cats, we stopped at a Wendy's, and I went in to get our lunch to go while Jenny stayed in the car with Sammy. We did insist that Sammy get out and stretch his legs, however.

After lunch we continued on our journey toward Lumberton. Eventually, we stopped at a Wawa for gas and another bite to eat. They have subs and other food choices and snacks of all kinds. There were tables outside, so we got Sammy out of the car so he could be near us while we ate. We left his cape and tie in the car so as to not draw attention to him. We just wanted to eat quietly.

We heard a few people comment on his size and say how cute he is. Otherwise, we were left alone.

"Well, I guess we'd better get moving," said Jenny.

"I'm ready for another nap," replied Sammy.

Once again we put Sammy back into his carrier and got into the car. Jenny turned the radio on, found a station that played soft music so Sammy could fall asleep. By the way, Jenny hates soft music. She and I argue about that all the time.

Chapter 6

Mom's New Car

Sammy liked his mom's new car better than the van. He didn't feel so far away from her in the back seat. He even felt more secure. The van was bigger, and he felt too far away from his mom when he rode in it. It gave him the feeling of being in a wide open space.

The new car was a KIA Soul, and it was more compact, so Sammy was actually closer to his mom. After all, cats like closed in spaces.

"Hey, Mom. This is a nice ride. I don't feel lost in a big space like I did in your van."

"Wow! You never told me that before, Sammy." Jenny was shocked.

"Well, the van was your car. You liked it. What could I say? I didn't want to upset you, Mom."

That was a lot for Jenny to digest. She had never thought about it before.

We rode in silence for a while. Then Jenny turned the radio on to a music station we both liked. I checked on Sammy. He had gone to sleep.

I forgot to mention that Jenny had a magnetic sign made for the car – Sammy, The Talking Cat. It was on the driver's door. I guess that's why some drivers blew their horns when they passed us. Some people waved. I waved back. It was fun.

So far we were having a delightful trip. Sammy seemed to enjoy himself between naps.

Chapter 7

Carol Is Allergic

As we approached the sign for Warrenton, VA, Sammy woke up. He yawned and stretched. When he saw the Warrenton sign, he said, "Hey! That's where the other famous Sammy lives. Can we stop and meet him?"

"That would be a wonderful idea, Sammy, except we don't have his address along, and your mother and I have no idea where he lives. I'm really sorry. We should have talked with his mom. I don't have her number along either."

"Shucks. I wanted to meet him. I understand he loves bacon. I've never tasted bacon."

"Maybe we'll plan a trip another time so you two can meet," Jenny said.

"It needs to be on a Saturday because that's when his mom makes bacon," replied Sammy.

And on down the road we went. Warrenton was not one of our regular stops on the trip to Lumberton.

We continued driving through Virginia. Jenny said it might be good to stop at our usual place in Fredericksburg to get gas, stretch, and take a restroom break. Sammy also thought that was a good idea.

When we arrived at the gas station, I went in and paid so Jenny could pump the gas. Sammy sat in his carrier and watched. After she finished pumping gas, Jenny moved the car closer to the store in order to free the gas pump for other customers.

We took turns using the restroom and getting drinks and snacks. After that was accomplished, Jenny put the leash on Sammy and got him out of the car so he could stretch his legs. He also found a spot to pee. Now, this is a litter box boy, so he was not accustomed to relieving himself outside.

After a little while, Jenny said it was time to hit the road. At this point we got on I 95 South and headed toward Richmond. We had a long way to go.

We passed the time talking and listening to music while Sammy slept. Occasionally, I nodded off as well. I awoke just as we reached Richmond.

"Let's wave to our friends, Carol and Bob as we go by their city. One of these days we'll have to stop and visit with them and spend the night. Carol brings it up every time I mention going to Lumberton," I said.

"Well , we can't stop on this trip because Carol is allergic to cats," Jenny replied.

This news did not sit well with Sammy. "I'm sorry. Is there anything I can do to help change that?"

"No, Sammy. I'm afraid not."

This news seemed to make him sad. He was pensive for a long time and then finally spoke.

"You mean all the Shaklee supplements she takes don't overcome this? What a shame, especially since I'm such a good boy. I know she would like me. And I'm famous too."

"I know, Sammy," I said. "There are things the supplements don't help me with also."

It wasn't long until we had passed Richmond.

Chapter 8

Cats Are Meat Eaters

Next came Petersburg, Virginia. At Exit 171, there is a Wendy's where we usually stop and eat. Carolina BBQ is also there. We always debate over the two and end up going the cheaper route. Today was no exception.

Usually, we eat inside Wendy's. We sit at one of those high tables. We've had good luck at this restaurant. The food is always good.

Sammy wanted us to go and sit inside for a change. He said he would be okay. He could sleep in his carrier. His mom and I were reluctant to leave him. Our distrust was not Sammy, but any passerby with ill intentions.

We both finally told him NO. One of us would stay in the car. Jenny asked the silly boy if he would like a small hamburger. I thought I'd fall over laughing.

"What? Cats are meat eaters."

"Yes, but has Sammy ever eaten a hamburger?" I asked.

"Well, no, but Jasper ate Turkey."

We both looked at Sammy. He just rolled his eyes and shook his head. "You two are a trip."

Jenny did not want to eat in the car, so we took turns going into Wendy's to eat. I thought Sammy should stretch his legs again, so we put the leash back on and got him out of the car for a short walk. He was getting a bit stiff, so this helped.

He also wanted to eat and drink some water – not too much though because we didn't want him to get car sick.

As everyone finished eating and got back into the car, we knew our next major stop would be the Welcome Center in North Carolina. As you can see, we were eating our way south.

Chapter 9

North Carolina Welcome Center

"There it is! Wake up Sammy!"

"What?" came a sleepy reply.

"The North Carolina Welcome Center. This is a major stop. I've put bookmarks with the picture of your book in here. They will be happy to meet you."

"Okay, but let me stretch and walk around and wake up first."

"Sammy, we are in North Carolina. We just have to drive through the state to get to Lumberton," Jenny said.

"Oh, boy! Oh, boy! I'm waking up now. North Carolina. Lumberton. Oh, boy." Sammy was excited.

Well, he could hardly contain his excitement. We got him out of his carrier, leash on, and walked him around. Jenny even took a picture of him by the welcome sign.

"Do you want to wear your cape and tie?" I asked.

"No. I just want fresh air. When I go inside, if I'm not wearing that stuff, they can see my nice shiny coat. Besides, I get hot wearing that."

After about five minutes, Sammy said he was ready to go inside. I went ahead and asked permission to bring him in. The nice lady who bought my Holocaust book was working.

I told her my name. Yes, she remembered me. Then I told her about Sammy's book and said that Sammy was outside and wanted to meet her.

"Of course. Bring him in. I love cats. And he's a celebrity."

So I went back outside and told Jenny to bring him in.

The lady at the counter was overjoyed. She called to her co-workers in the office to come and meet the famous cat.

Sammy purred and purred as everyone petted him and said how beautiful he was. Sammy just smiled. The lady asked if she could hold him.

"Of course," said Jenny, "but don't hurt your back. He's heavy."

"Oh, my goodness! You are a big boy," exclaimed the lady. Sammy looked at her and smiled and said, "Yes, I am." At this everyone laughed.

She gave him back to Jenny who put him down. He asked to walk around and look at the displays and nice furniture. Yes, Aunt Judy also likes the furniture. It is all from North Carolina furniture showrooms. She especially likes the upholstered chairs.

Finally, it was time to leave. We still had a ways to go before we reached our destination: Lumberton.

Exits 17-22

New York 626

Richmond 340

95

74

LUMBERTON

Charleston 166

95

Orlando 501

Miami 710

Chapter 10

The Final Destination

After we left the Welcome Center, the trip through North Carolina was pretty uneventful. The countryside was very flat and often swampy. We stopped a few times to take potty breaks and walk Sammy. He needed some exercise also.

At one point he noticed the swampy areas beside the road and asked if it was safe for him to be outside the car. We assured him that we would not let anything happen to him. We also stopped only at places that looked very safe.

After each break, Sammy went back to sleep. We knew he liked to take afternoon naps. And so did I. Jenny played the radio to help her stay awake. After all, she was the driver.

Eventually, we started seeing mileage signs to Lumberton. It had been a long day, and we were all anxious to reach our destination. Finally, we saw the exit signs for Lumberton.

We had booked a room at the Country Inn and Suites right off I 95 at Exit 20. That's where we stay when we come to Lumberton for the Book'Em North Carolina book festival. We had gotten permission for Sammy to stay with us when we booked the room.

We also declined room service for the safety of Sammy. We did not plan to keep him in his carrier, and we couldn't risk his getting out of the room if a stranger entered.

We got off the exit and Jenny parked in front of the hotel so I could go in and register and get a baggage cart. Since we were only staying one night, Jenny and I shared a suitcase. We also put Sammy's carrier (with him in it) on the cart along with his litter box and all of his essentials. Jenny wanted to make it in one trip.

I forgot to mention that I woke Sammy just as we got to Lumberton. Needless to say, he was quite excited.

After I checked in, we brought the cart inside the lobby. I stayed with it while Jenny parked the car. Then we got on the elevator to go upstairs to our room. When the elevator started moving, Sammy looked at us with concern in his eyes. I assured him that all was well and we would be off the elevator very soon.

I had rented a suite because this would give Sammy more room to exercise. There were two rooms and a bath.

The one was a sitting room with a couch, two chairs, TV, and a table with two chairs. There is also a TV in the bedroom. It also has a refrigerator. Since there are two queen beds, Sammy will be able to choose to share his mom's or mine. I'm sure he will pick Jenny's. Since it is a strange place to him, he will probably wander around half the night.

Chapter 11

Party at the Restaurant

After we had unpacked and freshened up, we got Sammy ready to go to the Village Station and meet some friends. Arnold, the owner had agreed to give us the back room so that Sammy would not be near the public and the buffet. After all, only seeing eye dogs are normally allowed in restaurants.

In addition to Arnold, several other friends would be there also. Lacey also had permission to bring her poodle, Puffin. We felt she and Sammy would get along because Sammy had adored Brittany, the spaniel, when she was alive.

Jenny put Sammy in his carrier and we drove to the Village Station. Sammy wanted to walk in, but we felt it would be best if he stayed in his carrier until we reached the back room.

Arnold hugged us when we walked in. He said he was anxious to meet the famous Sammy. We all walked to the back room, except Sammy who was still in his carrier and had to be carried.

Lacey and her husband and Puffin were waiting for us. Samantha and her friend Sally were there. Even the manager of our hotel had been invited. Pearl, Franny, and Carla had made the trip as well. Trish came over and hugged us. She was delighted to see us. Trish is the one who introduced us to Lumberton several years ago by organizing the first book show. Kathy from the library was also there.

It was time for Jenny to put Sammy's leash on and take him out of his carrier.

"Wow! What a big cat!" exclaimed Lacey. "Why, he's bigger than Puffin."

Kathy wanted to hold him. Sammy purred for her. Trish petted him and said, "So he's the one who started Judy's cat books. I see his name every year on the sales log."

Sammy was in his glory. Arnold came over and said, "Let me hold this big man." Sammy went to him right away.

"Whoa. He is heavy. What does he weigh?" asked Arnold.

"Around 23 pounds," said Jenny. "He had weighed more, but I've had him on a diet. He prefers the eat and sleep diet, but the vet wants him to lose some weight. It's a battle. Food makes him happy."

"Can I give him some chicken or beef from the buffet?" asked Arnold.

"You'd better ask him," Jenny replied.

"Maybe he'd like the salmon. Most cats like salmon. Here. You take Sammy and I'll get a small plate with some salmon. I'll be right back, big boy."

With that Arnold handed him to Jenny and left the room.

Although the party was for him, Sammy didn't have much to say. He was tired from the long road trip.

Soon Arnold returned with a small plate of salmon for Sammy. Jenny put him down and let him sniff the plate. To our amazement, Sammy devoured the salmon.

Finally, he spoke. "Boy, that was good! Why don't you give me that at home, Mom?"

"Arnold, I think you started something." Jenny said.

Arnold just laughed. In order to be fair, he asked Lacey what she thought Puffin would eat.

"Oh, she likes chicken, but no bones."

"I'll prepare a plate for her. She's such a good dog and so beautiful."

"Yes, she's our pride and joy and our little angel."

Everyone took turns petting and holding the two animals. Now, it was time for the featured book signing.

Arnold's staff had brought in a table for me to display Sammy and his book. Jenny went out to the car and brought in his poster and a container of <u>Sammy, The Talking Cat</u>. We covered the table with a cloth, positioned the poster and books. Jenny also placed Sammy on the table.

I sat behind the table ready to autograph books people purchased. Arnold went out to the dining room and told patrons there was a book signing in the back room along with the famous talking cat.

Quite a few people came back to meet Sammy. He was in his glory. He told them to be sure and buy his book. He even asked one man if he could talk on his cell phone. That created a stir of laughter. Almost everyone bought his book.

Afterwards, Arnold told us that the buffet would be half price for our group tonight in honor of Sammy's celebrity status. Arnold is such a gracious man.

Sammy said he was tired and asked if he could lie down in his carrier and take a nap while we ate and talked. So, Jenny put him in his carrier where he curled up and went to sleep.

We spent the next hour or so eating and talking. We absolutely loved the buffet.

Finally, it was time to leave the party. We paid our bill, thanked Arnold, and said good-night to everyone.

Back at the hotel, Sammy promptly used his litter box and then asked which bed was his mom's. He wanted to go to bed. He had had a big day, and he was a very tired boy.

The next morning Jenny and I enjoyed breakfast in the hotel dining room. Sammy stayed upstairs and slept.

After a relaxing morning at the hotel, we headed out to one of our favorite lunch places in Lumberton – Smithfield's. It is a fast food, bar-b-que chicken joint. We discovered it a couple of years ago. The sandwiches are great, and they have Coke. This made me happy because I am a Coke drinker.

To our disappointment, Smithfield's was closed for renovation. Sammy was disappointed also because we had promised him some chicken. Instead, we went to Wendy's for a hamburger. Sammy said he'd pass and just eat his own food.

It was now time to return to the hotel and collect our belongings and begin the long trip home. Sammy had seen Lumberton.

Sammy says, "Thank you for going on this tour with me. I loved meeting so many friends and fans. It was a fun trip and I loved every minute of it, but it sure is nice being back home and sleeping in my own bed."

Love, Sammy

Other books by Judy S. Walter

Nightmare In Europe
Sammy, The Talking Cat
The Grey and White Stranger
Life With Mitzi
The Dog From York and Other Stories
Simple Book Marketing
The Escape Artist – A Collection of
                    Poems and Essays

About the Author

A retired English teacher, Judy S. Walter is a substitute teacher and the author of numerous books for children and adults, including a collection of poetry and essays. She resides in PA.

Made in the USA
Middletown, DE
01 October 2017